Rescued From Time

Also by Barbara Fisher
Archival Footwork
Still Life, Other Life
Rain and Hirohito

Barbara Fisher
Rescued From Time

Acknowledgements

Thanks are due to the editors of the following publications
in which many of these poems first appeared:
*Australian Poetry Journal, Famous Reporter, Eucalypt,
Meanjin, Quadrant*

Barbara Fisher is represented in the following anthologies:
The Best Australian Poems 2004 (Black Inc.)
The Best Australian Poems 2006 (Black Inc.)
The Best Australian Poetry 2007 (UQP)
When the Sky Caught Fire – Youngstreet Poets Anthology 8 (2008)
Grevillea & Wonga Vine – Australian Tanka of Place (Eucalypt, 2011)
The Quadrant Book of Poetry (2012)
Women's Work (Pax Press, 2013)
This Strange World – Youngstreet Poets Anthology 9 (2013)

Rescued From Time
ISBN 978 1 76041 233 3
Copyright © text Barbara Fisher 2016
Cover image: Grace Cossington Smith, *Door to the Garden*, © Estate
of Grace Cossington Smith, used by permission
Cover design: Alex Baird

First published 2016 by
GINNINDERRA PRESS
PO Box 3461 Port Adelaide 5015 Australia
www.ginninderrapress.com.au

Contents

I — 9
- Deckchairs — 11
- The Proper Spirit — 12
- Conversations I Do Not Have — 13
- Kristallnacht — 15
- At Breakfast — 16
- On Looking at Ghirlandaio's Portrait … — 17
- Glass Flowers — 18
- Remembering Moscow — 20
- Coming Home — 22
- Hospital Vistas — 24
- Historic House Visit — 26
- Conversions — 27

II — 29
- In Praise of Oranges — 31
- Lunch In the Garden — 32
- Paperbarks — 33
- Casuarinas — 34
- Palms — 36
- By the Lake — 37
- Birds Bathing — 38
- Bush Lemons — 40
- Light – Late Afternoon — 41
- Lake George — 42

III — 43
- A Colonial Story — 45

IV — 57
- Snapshot — 59
- Leaf Shadows — 60

In the Picture	61
Lost Uncles	62
Nursing Home	63
Evening	64
Tears	66
Dream	67
Skiing In the Main Range	68
Forgetting	70
To an Adopted Child	71
Plastic Flowers	72
Viewpoints	73
Sydney To Melbourne	75
Place Dauphine	76

V   79

Toast	81
A Survivor	83
White	84
Red	85
Blue	86
Yellow	87
Optimism	88
Mushrooms	89
Turkish Dessert	90
Ten Tanka	91
Grace Cossington Smith's Interiors	93
Considering Fred Williams's Landscapes	94
Postcards	95
Shrine	96

VI   97

Fragments of a Life	99

in memory of John

and for Patrick and Lucy and their families

'Art, in a sense, is life brought to a standstill, rescued from time.'
– James Salter, *Burning the Days: Recollections*

I

Deckchairs

It seems these canvas contraptions are coming back,
have been sighted in modish homewares stores,
along with designer cushions and every sort of throw.

Deckchairs! Those favourites of the 1930s,
supporting all those Bloomsbury bottoms
in drowsy summer gardens of the literati.

The famous faces look up at the camera –
Vanessa and Clive and the Woolves, Morgan,
Lytton and Carrington – from panamas,

early sunglasses or thatch of remarkable hair.
Because they are sitting so close to the ground
they seem vulnerable, yet how steadily

photographs record their confident gaze;
we guess the witticism just uttered, the laughter
dissolving in the mild, tobacco-scented air.

The Proper Spirit

Actors always say the clothes they wear on stage
do more than make them look the part,
they make them feel it in their flesh and bones.
So the man in doublet, hose and cloak,
puts on courtliness with every garment,
or with the weight of a long greatcoat
heavy on his shoulders, will assume *gravitas*
or find himself with a different step induced
by military boots and cane. He may need
to exercise an arm in the etiquette of the hat
or even know the pinch of a clerical collar
around his unaccustomed neck.

Women are well acquainted with the constraints
of costume – tight-laced stays, the upward push
of breasts, the tug of heavy skirts or swaying walk
occasioned by a crinoline. Or moving into drama
of the kitchen sink variety, may understand
the scrape of scalp with hair pulled into curlers,
the flattening of feet in pompommed slippers
– easy to imagine the incipience of bunions…

But Mr and Mrs William Blake considered clothes
in a different light. One summer afternoon the couple
were discovered sitting at ease in their garden
reading *Paradise Lost*. Both had taken off their clothes,
believing nakedness would encourage the proper spirit
in which to appreciate that great work.

Conversations I Do Not Have

For some time I have been wanting to tell a friend
she looks rather like Queen Mary.
All she needs is a toque, a long dress, pearls –
a great many of them – and a furled parasol
but I don't say this because I don't think she'd like it
and certainly wouldn't approve of the Queen's habit
of embarrassing her hosts into parting
with their prized antiques. And my friend
would take a dim view of anyone who collected Fabergé.
So that is one conversation, admittedly trivial,
which I do not have.

Another conversation disallowed is when I'm a guest at dinner
and find on the table what looks like a dead fish.
Pallid and moist, it is actually a moulded concoction
involving a tin of tuna and a great deal of effort
but the effect is irretrievably of something on a mortuary slab,
which no profusion of sliced lemon can dispel.
Clearly, praise is expected. Cravenly I oblige,
with words as bland as I know the thing will taste.

Christmases and birthdays are challenging of that
which must remain unsaid. The ribbons cut,
the wrappings dropped in bright confusion on the floor
and the dreaded garment held aloft for the white lies
of gratitude – as I remember the book I cannot read,
the earrings I will never wear and the nougat I dislike.

Funerals also impose their discipline and sometimes stupefaction.
Who was this man they eulogise? I do not think I knew
this *loving husband* – selfish and obsessed with golf,
or that *devoted father*, whose children couldn't wait to leave home,
not to mention *generous to a fault* – who never had a wallet
when the time came to pay the bill.

Oh let me speak of weather! That is surely safer,
so easy to agree the wind is fresh and yes, it looks like rain
but on hearing that a cold snap is predicted
I do not dare to voice the hope that I will wake next day
to Sydney's freakish fall of snow.
From my window, through drifting flakes,
I'll find familiar townscape in a white disguise,
leafless trees redrawn with snow and parked cars
softly blanketed, all traffic stilled, the silence absolute.

Kristallnacht

That German flair for poetry!
If you didn't know you could picture
some old autumn festival…
Darling children,
soon it will be Kristallnacht
and all the kristall fairies
are bringing sugarplums
for every child that's good.
Candles lit in windows,
processions in the streets
and smell the roasting chestnuts
in the frosty air!
Such a pity to remember
Night of Broken Glass,
the other name
for that November night
of smashing Jewish windows
and setting fire to synagogues.
Odd that in Bayreuth
the synagogue survived.
Had decency prevailed
in Wagner's town? Not so.
Its saviour was a theatre –
they could not risk a fire
so close to this rococo gem.

At Breakfast

In Jacob Jansz's painting,
circa fifteen hundred,
a family is seated at table
on which are breads, a jug
and something that could be cheese.

It looks as though the wife
is wearing her best clothes –
a dress of red brocade,
a matching shawl and a fancy cap
with trimmings of gold braid.

The child on her lap is pale
with an old head on his shoulders.
He looks as though he needs
some feeding up – perhaps whatever
his mother is spooning from a cup.

The husband is bearded and solemn,
plainly but carefully dressed
and gravely intent on slicing
a loaf of pumpernickel which
he holds in both his hands.

This placid picture of a meal
hangs in a gallery in Cologne
and gives us a rare glimpse
of the Holy Family sitting down
to a very German breakfast.

On Looking at Ghirlandaio's Portrait of an Old Man and his Grandson

Yes, the old man's nose
is the first thing we notice.
Undeniably ugly, it is very large
and covered with warts, cruel contrast
to his grandson's upturned face
with its flawless skin and golden hair.
But then our perception shifts.
We start to see the old man
as his grandson sees him,
we catch that faint smile
and the tenderness as his hooded eyes
look down on the radiant child
pressed against him.
Both their clothes are the same warm red,
as if to reflect the blood that binds them
and the more we look at them
we know something marvellous
is alive in the work.

Glass Flowers

Harvard's Botanical Museum
has all the quiet
of a place where interactive exhibitions
are unknown.
No buttons to push,
no warm-voiced spiel of information,
not even an attendant in sight.
Our footsteps are the only sound.

Botanical examples are displayed
in rows of glass cases –
every sort of plant and all
miraculously made of wire
and coloured glass,
scientifically accurate,
surmounting the constraints
of climate and geography
New England could impose
on living specimens.
So delicate a contradiction
takes the breath away –
slender stalks and tender leaves,
a frail translucency of petals,
meticulously fashioned seed pods,
fruits, a fine mesh of roots,
sometimes a pollinating insect.
Yet if we could touch them
we'd be rewarded with solidity,
marble-hard yet fragile in its cool perfection.

Who could make this magic?
Only, it seems, the Blaschkas,*
who left no children nor apprentices
and whose Dresden workshop
was hit by a bomb
at the end of the second World War.
It is so quiet in the museum,
quiet as a petal
falling to the floor.

---

*The Blaschkas, father Leopold (1822–1895) and son Rudolf (1853–1939), established themselves in Dresden as scientific glass artists of distinction. From 1890 until 1937, they worked exclusively for the Botanical Museum at Harvard University, producing over 3,000 models of 164 plant varieties. 'Glass Flowers' is the popular name for this remarkable collection.

Remembering Moscow

What do I remember
of Moscow?
Not enough probably.
I never knew exactly where the hotel was
in relation to sights seen –
Red Square unbelievably huge,
onion domes of many colours
and the Kremlin chock-full
of cathedrals.
The chance too of one's photo taken
with a convincing group of lookalikes,
Marx, Lenin and the last Tsar.
Oh, and the terrifying traffic.
But what I remember most
is wondering why the hotel dining room
was serving so many young couples,
American, each with a small child
at their table.
They did not seem like tourists,
were not surrounded with
the apparatus of happiness and yet
I later found they all were looking
for something more than that.
They were in the final stages
of the Byzantine process
of adopting a Russian orphan.

A radiant couple in the lift
cradled their new daughter
awash in drifts of pink.
Three years old, they said –
and I had thought her barely one.

Coming Home

Flying home on this November morning
a map has unrolled beneath us –
red earth and creamy lakes of salt,
merging into spinifex and roads
like wandering lengths of string.
We must have dozed, for waking
gives us paddocks of blond grass,
willowed creeks and ragged little towns.
Soon we are skimming soft mattresses of cloud,
which sometimes part to offer views
of fold on fold of olive-scumbled bush,
until the probe of many-fingered waterways
signals our descent. At last we see
the green ocean below, breakers frilled
with foam, yet seeming not to move –
a trick of distance that also spreads
a vast mosaic of suburbs – tesserae
of terracotta, turquoise swimming pools
and the bruised blue of jacarandas.

A weary gathering up of things,
the waiting at the carousel, remembered voices
with their wide vowels, and the easy good nature
of nothing to declare. Our taxi driver
comes from Piraeus, has a pocket-sized icon
on his dashboard and a photo of his family.
He wonders if we've been to Greece.

How empty the house smells!
Rooms seem smaller and ceilings lower.
Someone has filled a vase with flowers,
put bread on the kitchen bench
and milk in the fridge.
We drink our tea on the veranda
and Europe slides off us. We know
we're back in the land of clear light
and freshly painted mornings,
with lorikeets weaving colours through the trees.

Hospital Vistas

1.

Waking early to an indigo sky,
yellow roses on my windowsill
have absorbed the night,
are silhouettes now
against the drift of dawn
as a transformation scene
plays out its alchemy –
a gradual flood of apricot
fills the sky, revives
the golden flowers and leaves
a field of cloudless blue

2.

Cumuli clouds this morning,
flushed pink and edged with gold,
stage set for a baroque swirl
of female flesh – limbs and breasts,
floating tresses and some helmeted hero
rising naked from a storm
of discreet drapery…
The vision fades. A nurse
has come to check blood pressure
and take my temperature.

3.

This afternoon, geography of cloud,
vast map of some forgotten land,
country of myth and fable,
home to dragons, unicorns,
with its unexplored coast and wandering sea,
distant mountain ranges,
all dissolving now in mist.
Rain is streaming down my windowpane.

4.

Birds wheel against a polar sky,
furrowed fields of snow, cliffs of ice,
a white nothingness to chill the heart.
I am just going outside and may be some time…
I fall asleep.

5.

Now that I can sit up the sky shrinks,
reveals the as yet empty roof
of the hospital car park
and the lift tower with its steel ladder
curving over the parapet.
I am in a painting by Jeffrey Smart,
complete with street lamp lifted
surely from an autostrada.
And can that tiny distant figure
be David Malouf, or is it Clive James?
Be that as it may, they are both welcome.
I drink my tea.

Historic House Visit

Professor Fletcher (Leeds and Cambridge),
with his rich voice and grubby collar,
enduring a holiday with his wife,
parted reluctantly with his dollar
and trailed his spouse from room to room,
absent-minded, bored and cross.
If the wretched place went up in smoke
he thought it would be no great loss.
The constant murmur of *solid cedar*
increased his irritation. It was odd
in this country how that sibilant refrain
seemed a sort of substitute for God.

This is the master bedroom, the guide intoned,
*Note the sumptuous four-poster, original
hangings still intact…*

Professor Fletcher in his mind's eye
his Ariadne seized, flung on the bed,
with all her loveliness arrayed
as if for his own banquet spread.
Swiftly he drew the curtains round
and fell upon her radiant flesh, then,
pleasure done, they'd drift to sleep
and wake to blissful lust again.
So it might be he mused, recalling
motel rooms and carpet-smelling air,
their clothes on hangers side by side,
and Ariadne, naked, brushing her hair.

Conversions

Who would think that charming kiosk on the harbour,
so elegantly roofed and garnished with a flêche
was once a lavatory for gents? Now it is an oyster bar,
prime position at the Quay, where patrons can enjoy
their Sydney Rocks to the slap of waves and moving light
of the water at their feet. And consider those old factories
where they made jam and condiments – now spacious
loft apartments, mimicking their cousins in New York.
We are beginning to embrace conversions.

The primary school's become a centre for senior citizens,
the church of the Holy Name was turned into a restaurant,
while rumour has it that the presbytery next door is eyed
by the owner of a brothel now that her rented premises
are earmarked for a refuge for homeless single mothers.
Reassuring though to know that whatever goes around
eventually does come around, for a fish shop at a bus stop
in a busy suburban street has been completely gutted
by a council keen to provide more public conveniences.

A postscript should be noted in this history of change.
The brothel madam has not pursued the presbytery idea;
business talks with the agent led to talks with Father Flynn,
who saw a soul to save. Now she is considering
a different career, which may involve her own conversion
and ultimate reception in the arms of mother church.

II

In Praise of Oranges

Comfort me with apples, cried the lovesick girl
(apricots, some scholars now maintain). Myself,
I would be happier with oranges. Can any fruit
surpass those juicy orbs, lambent in the dark green
of their leafage? But I am prejudiced. Four years old,
they let me loose to play in the orange grove
that lapped my aunt's old house with tides of trees
and as far as I could see. Alone and quite content
I walked those glossy rows, deep in a game
of going to school. I don't remember *eating* oranges,
only the wonder of those avenues, the long perspectives
of rounded, laden trees.

The pleasures of eating oranges and methods of approach
came later: the unbroken coil of peel from dextrous hands,
the careful division of segments; the quarters children suck,
then fill their mouths with leering teeth cut from the skin;
halves prepared like grapefruit and eaten with a spoon;
perfect slices shorn of pith, brandied and strewn with shards
of caramel. And what of sauces – Bigarade, Maltese,
or the delights of crêpes Suzette and orange almond cake?

The smell of oranges is something I'll not forget.
First whiff and I'm climbing the stairs to that London flat
we lived in years ago. Our landlord has opened a case
of oranges from Jaffa, a present he does not share.
But their perfume lifts the fug of the darkening hall
and follows my ascent, full of sunshine and tangy sweetness
with memories of warmth – gift enough in the cold
of a damp February afternoon.

Lunch In the Garden

How still is the life on that table set
for lunch in the garden? The white cloth spread,
knives and forks, a basket of fruit,
ham and salad, cheese and bread,
still life indeed and fixed in place, yet
when a breeze disturbs the shade
of a stand of casuarinas, splintered light
seems to put everything in flight.

Holding up my glass, a flash of olive green
and yellow tells me I've just seen
a lorikeet speed to his favourite tree,
callistemon linearis – but bottlebrush to me,
where, feasting on the crimson flowers
he'll stretch his lunch for many hours.

But I will lock this garden meal away
in grateful memory, marvel at the play
of moving light and a brilliant bird on the wing
and that brief moment – shimmering.

Paperbarks

Such comfortable trees, those old melaleucas.
They look at themselves on the shores of lakes,
or get their feet wet in treacle-brown creeks.

You see them too in suburban avenues.
With their generous wrappings of loose bark
they make me think of ancient relatives

in shabby dressing gowns, shuffling
to bed with hot-water bottles, milky drinks
and a book to put them to sleep.

Paperbarks welcome climbing children
with obligingly low boughs, don't mind
if they peel off the pastel, papery layers,

so soft in the hand. But it's summertime
when their kindness knows no bounds
and those creamy clouds of blossom

hum with bees and smell of warm honey.

Casuarinas

The name casuarina, from the Malay Kasuari, alludes to the similarity of the drooping foliage of the genus to the feathers of the cassowary bird.

Sometimes people call them she-oaks, or river oaks,
remembering large stately trees on the banks
of freshwater streams, soft smudges against the sky,

their feathery foliage a shadowy greenish grey.
They stand on mattresses of fallen needles
scattered with their tiny bead-like cones.

Our soundless tread's so different from the crack
and snap of walking through dry bush and scrub
we almost feel we should lower our voices.

They're accommodating trees, will grow
in sandy loam, in alkaline and brackish soils,
serve as windbreaks, avenues and tactful screens

for suburban bus depots and power stations.
The branchlets of some species will feed stock
in times of drought, while the wood is dense and hard.

Is there no end to the virtues of the genus casuarina?
How easy to ascribe a feminine persona
to this paragon of trees, graceful yet adaptable,

nurturing and practical, provider in the past
of timber for shingles, bullock yokes, axe handles.
Even as fuel it is sublime for when it's burnt

is almost smokeless; in the days when every town
made its own bread, bakers loved it for their ovens.
If I had never heard of the flightless bird

that gave us casuarina I surely would invent
my own associated saint, one Santa Casuarina,
patron of equanimity, comfort and domestic order,

(soft bedding, good fires and well-baked bread).
I see her like Saint Barbara – of pious legend,
dropped from the Vatican calendar but still
revered in certain parts, regardless of the Holy See.

Palms

Not all are favoured for resorts. Exotics
are preferred, although they've tried
the native cabbage-tree – its very name strikes

a homely note, discouraging to developers.
It's a disobliging tree with scruffy underpinnings
to its crown, quite out of place on patios

or grouped beside the swimming-pool,
a bit like poor relations at a smart party.
These are workaday palms, providers once

of hats for colonists and a ready supply
of kindling from their dry, discarded fans
strewn on the ground below.

The *phoenix canariensis* is another escapee
from resort land, popular once with its
fountain of fronds and trunk like a pineapple,

star of old suburban gardens with buffalo
lawns, paths of concrete painted red
and moon-faced dahlias lashed to stakes.

They were favourites too in municipal parks,
with cannas and conveniences, bandstand
and the war memorial soldier.

But Palm Sunday is their finest hour,
when cut and carried in procession
they show how memory of that ride
transcends all time and place.

By the Lake

A sunless day and coolish. No weather
for a picnic. We have parked by the lake
and are eating our sandwiches in the car.

It's one of those melancholy days when lake
and sky are the same grey; even the trees,
paperbarks mostly, offer only variations of tone.

The whole scene looks as though it's composed
of fabrics: silk, faintly wrinkled, for the great
stretch of water, dark stitching for distant

oyster leases, with here and there embroidery
of black swans, while the folded, bush-clad hills
present a sombre tangle of knitting wool.

The cloudy sky is a vast cashmere shawl
– but here the fantasy begins to falter,
for looking at the big picture, we've failed

to notice modest runabouts the fishermen
have moored not far offshore, and suddenly
we realise they are crammed (appliquéd?)

with pelicans, four or five to a boat,
taking their ease, silent, companionable,
as if they're waiting for latecomers before

setting out on their party of pleasure.

Birds Bathing

The bird bath on our balcony
has many visitors.
Two floors up at tree-top level,
discreetly screened by potted shrubs
and safe from predators,
it seems as if the birds have found
a sort of Baden-Baden
where they can drink and bathe.

Noisy miners wing in
usually in pairs, nervous
in their attitude to getting wet.
In they hop for a second,
then as quickly out,
with finicky flapping
to dry themselves
before they plunge again –
a performance they repeat
sometimes thirteen times.

Different the solitary currawong.
He comes first for a drink.
A slow sip, then his yellow eyes
are skyward, lost in some reflection.
Now and then, although too big,
he takes a bath and a tidal wave
slaps over the rim,
sloshing the balcony floor.

Before the lorikeets venture our resort
they socialise in the trees, colours
bouncing in leafage as they maintain
a non-stop conversation. Bathing together
they wallow, water up to their necks,
so their olive greens and yellows, scarlets
and ultramarines seem freshly painted,
shining, dripping wet.

Bush Lemons

Once there was a vineyard here
in green and ordered rows.
Now the bleaching grasses bend
and nothing fruitful grows

except a self-sown lemon tree
with leprous, aching boughs,
heavy with the bitter fruit
come of a daze of flowers.

Strange, ugly and unpromising fruit,
a crop of warted noses,
nothing you present to view
your secret good discloses,

how soaked and simmered long
with drifts of sugar stirred,
you foam and bubble and become
the robust marmalade preferred

by those who scorn the sweeter kind
and in your lucent depths behold
treasure of housewifely sort,
apotheosis, dross to gold.

Light – Late Afternoon

How they loved late afternoon,
those painters we love too,
limning landscapes in a vein

of mild romanticism,
all honeyed light and limpid skies,
pools of shadow and, picked out

with dabs of colour, tiny figures,
a boy driving sheep perhaps,
wearing his vermilion jacket,

or some young girl in a straw hat
– a touch of Naples yellow –
bringing in the cows, their flanks

catching the last of the sun.
Almost one hears their lowing
and the stir of birds busy

with evening arrangements
before the light has gone.

*

In my late afternoon an open door
has trapped a path of sunlight
on the polished floor.

Curtains, chairs, table are warmed
in the last rays and the bowl of mandarins
is burning with a steady fire.

Lake George

They call it the disappearing lake,
sometimes there but often not:
a sheet of water when rains are good,
welcome sight from the highway
some forty ks from Canberra –
or just low-lying paddocks
with grazing sheep and cattle,
a mystery to motorists who've seen
a sign proclaiming this mild pastoral
is actually a lake. To think
that in its glory days
it teemed with fish!

Once, driving by Lake George
we saw it *was* a lake and the distant shore
seemed like some foreign coast
seen faintly through the morning mist.
Ochre hills met shining water –
hard not to fantasise of frontiers
and other tongues, imagine towers
and gilded domes catching
the shifting sunlight, concoct a people
proud, remote, immersed in their affairs,
unaware of our national capital,
its suburban spread, unpeopled parkland,
statement-making embassies,
tourists lost in byways and public servants,
politicians, circling that mantis flagpole
in their white official cars.

III

A Colonial Story

1985

All that warm September day
people are moving through the great house,
heritage treasure of New South Wales:
Colonial Georgian, perfectly placed,
commanding views of park and garden,
still extensive in spite of suburbs
nibbling at the lodge and gates.
There was money – a great deal of it.
National Trust ladies are dispensing leaflets
on the history of the mansion and though
there is uncertainty as to architect,
there's none on furniture and pictures
with which the house is filled.
Experts have pronounced them very fine.
Out of respect for the last owner, a lady
only recently deceased, information
on the ancestor who built the pile
and made a fortune is somewhat vague.
No, he was not a convict.
He was an officer and a gentleman
but his death was a mystery.

National Trust ladies are hoping
that a tedious old retainer
lurking near the stables
is not waylaying visitors
with tales both vivid and unverified.

Ninety-five if a day, with few
remaining teeth, he's relishing the chance
to yarn, and who is to say him nay?
Only Miss Phillimore, Writer in Residence,
who likes old Jim but is always too busy
to listen to what he has to say.

2.

You haven't heard the story?
Well, it were hushed up, you know.
'Course the house was convict built,
they built 'em solid then. They don't
build like that today – nor keep poor buggers
in chains with bread and water tucker –
and they call them the good old days.
'Course they didn't have our conveniences,
none of your wall-to-wall
and pretty cold here of an evening
with a candle to your bed.
Well, Captain FitzGibbon –
you seen his picture in the house?
He come out here with his lady wife
and didn't much care for the place
for all that they said he was keen
on the flora and fauna and such,
him being by way of an artist
in a strictly botanical line.
Still, when he'd done up at the barracks
and marched a few convicts around,
time hung a bit heavy like.

His heart wasn't in it, you see,
but his head knew a thing or two.
Not many years and he's rich,
got himself this great place
and a carriage made special in London,
sailing the seas to the glory
of Captain FitzGibbon, his lady
and six little steps and stairs.
A fine sight it was of a Sunday,
my grandad used often to say,
to see 'em all going to church,
two thieves at the back for lackeys
and a murderer at the reins,
all dressed up in livery they were,
scarlet and gold, Grandad said.
Ting! Ting! went the little church bell
and the Captain, he would wince
like you'd trod on his little toe.
He was musical you know.

3.

'FitzGibbon, Arthur Edwin,
Captain in the 39th Regiment
arrived in Sydney Cove in 1827.'
Miss Phillimore lays down her pen
and looks again at the miniature –
the small neat head, thick black brows
and rather womanish mouth, the neck
half-throttled with fine linen stock,
red coat taut over spare little chest.

Miss Phillimore resumes:
'Younger son of Sir James FitzGibbon, Bart,
whose seat, Aston Park, in Devonshire,
is a fine example of Palladian architecture.
No surprise then that the house he built here
is a handsome colonial version
of this most elegant style.'

A knock on the door and the caretaker's wife
comes in with a cup of tea.
Miss Phillimore, Writer in Residence,
makes Mrs Jessop nervous.
Not that she gives any trouble,
is unfailingly polite, but there is
always a kind of sweet disdain
which is hard to put a finger on.
When Mrs Jessop once had said
she had to dust the lounge,
Miss Phillimore looked puzzled,
smiled and said,
'I think you mean the drawing room.'
And when she rashly offered
to lend the writer a book
Miss Phillimore looked askance
at the proffered *Women's Weekly*.

Eleanor Phillimore had fallen in love
with a house – and perhaps
with Captain FirzGibbon.

Friends spoke of Eleanor's obsession
and some remembered feeling crushed
if ever they queried her research,
a date, an attribution, and recalled
her scalding comment on any idea
that did not tally with her own.

4.

As the afternoon progressed and visitors
had had their fill of colonial splendour
they wandered to the stables, where
old Jim found himself the centre
of a clutch of listeners to the tale he loved to tell.

Now that bell is the thing I'm coming to,
that bell drove the Captain mad,
sounding so cheap-like, not fit to call
an officer's family, a baronet's son
to service of a Sunday. It got so the Captain
felt a fool whenever the bell was rung.
He'd be standing in his fine parlour
or drawing a bit of fern, when in chipped
that tinny old bell making mock of him.
Well, that's what he thought.

5.

Not that he mentioned this irritant
in the Arcadia he described
when he wrote to his sister-in-law,
widowed young but mother of a son.
She had preferred his elder brother
and the consequence of marriage
to a baronet than to a young man
of no fortune with his way to make
in the world. In letters unknown to his wife
he told of his growing prosperity
and the elegant house he had built,
the horses in his stables and the sheep
growing fat on his land.

I wish, Maria, he wrote, *that you could see
our gardens full of fruit and flowers
and the great avenue I have planted,
longer than at home, that leads up to the house.
Dearest Maria, all this might have had you
for a mistress. Why should I not torment you
as you tormented me?
Last night I hung in Charlotte's ears
diamonds you disdained, but all her smiles
I would disown for one of your tears…
Forgive me, dearest. I send you drawings
I have made of ferns and one of a waratah.*

Let me think of your dear head bent
over these offerings. Keep them, pray,
in your little desk beneath the window,
shut safe away. Write to me who loves you,
under separate cover, to the barracks.

6.

Lady FitzGibbon unlocked her desk
and put the drawings there.
She always burnt his letters
but wondered how it might have been
had things been otherwise. Better far,
she thought, to be the mother of the heir
to comfortable estates, enjoy her standing
in the county. She could not see herself
in New South Wales, set down
in the crude society that colonies supply.
She never wrote to the barracks,
confined herself to bland epistles
for reading in the family circle.

My dear Maria, wrote Mrs FitzGibbon,
We are tolerably settled now,
with the house improving every day.
Our gardens would make you smile,
so raw and set about with these odd native trees,
but Captain FitzGibbon has had laid out
an orchard and soon a grove of orange trees.

The children thrive – exhaustingly,
though Fanny has grown quieter and begs
to send her best love to her cousin.
I am often ill with the summer heat
and keep to my sofa, good for nothing,
but Captain FitzGibbon never feels it
so I get no sympathy from that quarter.
If only it was May and we were at the Park
said I one day at luncheon, when the butter
ran to oil and my head was near to bursting
with the noise of locusts singing,
but a black look, very stern,
was all the answer made.

7.

Old Jim was still holding forth,
enjoying his role of ancient retainer,
beguiling visitors looking for tea,
or a stroll in the gardens and a tour
of the ice-house and the dairy.
But Mrs Dunphy was not to be detained.
She'd seen the house and marvelled
at the lofty rooms – oh, the dusting!
But the gardens were what she wanted to see,
so beautifully laid out, she murmured
more to herself than husband Bob,
who was feeling bolshy and muttering
all this bloody privilege and old money,
never mind how you made it, not to mention
Colonial Georgian claptrap, said he was tired
and stomped off to the bus.

Left to herself, she noted the level lawns,
trees as tall as churches, a real herbaceous border
and on the kitchen garden wall, espaliered apples,
pears, just like the Hall when she was in service
at home. There was the same smell of sun
and herbs and warm straw on the strawberry beds.
The times she'd pinched a berry
from under the head gardener's nose!
'You'll catch it, Ethel,' her sister said,
'Your mouth is stained that red,'
and took one for herself.

'So you are off to Orstralia, Ethel?' Mrs Vane said.
'Yes, Madam, my sister and I, we sort of decided…'
But then the motor was heard on the gravel
and Mr Frank greeting young ladies –
always wild for him they were.
'Tea, I think, Ethel,' Mrs Vane smiled.
'We will speak of it later.'
Next thing, Ethel's bearing the laden tray
and surprised at her face so fat in the silver,
sets her load down with a crash and a storm
of muffins lobs in Mrs Vane's lap.
Shrieks and giggles, herself close to tears
and Madam most desperately sweet.
When the door closes, a voice slightly raised,
'Orstralia' and 'Ethel' and laughter in waves
washing her up the back stairs to sob
on her narrow white bed.

They never did talk of it later, could not believe
it was true. 'Ethel is seeking her fortune'
and jokes about kangaroos.

8.

One of the National Trust ladies,
seeing old Jim still at it, thought to silence him
with a cup of tea and a slice of cake
but her kindness only spurs him on
in the telling of his tale.

Now that tinny old bell drove the Captain mad,
so what does he do but order one special in England?
Costing a packet but who was he to care,
him being so rich a gentleman with his grand house
and carriage and pair? At last comes the Sunday
when the new bell's set up to be rung
for the very first time, and the folk in the district
awaiting. best bib and tuckers and all.
'Morning, Captain' and 'Good day to you, Ma'am'
as the fine FitzGibbon family make their way
to the belfry where the Captain's to pull
the spanking new rope and ring the first chime.
And so he does and the crowd sends up a cheer.
'What a sweet, pretty bell,' 'What a beautiful tone!'
'There's nothing so grand as a really good bell'
and 'God in His goodness and let us give thanks,'
with everyone smiling and glad.

*But the Captain's face is white, he's looking ill
but nobody knows what ails him. My grandad said
from that day on the Captain wasn't the same.
After that day things started to go downhill.
Folk said that after they'd got the new bell
the Captain wasn't pleased. It seemed he didn't
like the new bell, complained it sounded the same
as the old one he'd replaced. And when they told him
he was wrong he liked that even less. That's when
he started to drink and scared his family out of their wits.*

9.

He did not know how he survived the service.
All the drive home they were ringing the bell
and Charlotte is praising the sweetness of the sound.
How tell her he hears the self-same ting, the tinniness?
Ting! Ting! Ting! Why had nothing changed?
Listening, listening, his head on one side,
the days slid into weeks and the Captain's head
began to fill with bells, softly at first but tinny
and so much worse on Sunday he would not go
to church. They gradually got louder and made
so cruel a clanging that brandy did not seem
to answer. Walking one morning in the garden,
kookaburras laughed at him in chorus,
lizards, smiling, darted from his path
and turning suddenly he caught his dogs
in some joke made at his expense.

Ting! Ting! Ting! Would the ringing never cease
its endless mockery? He knew then what he had to do,
went swiftly to his study, took the case
that held his pistols and with a steady hand
dispatched himself and silenced the bells for ever.

10.

A tragic accident, Miss Phillimore had written,
as had his wife so many years before,
with talk of cleaning weapons and the dangers
of so doing; but there was other talk
that would not go away, of drinking and delusions,
sudden bursts of rage and random accusations
of laughter when his back was turned.
Miss Phillimore was adamant
that this was mindless gossip
and who's to say her nay?

IV

Snapshot

There are four of them in the photograph –
my father and mother and another young couple,
whose names I do not know.
It could be 1934 and the weather is warm,
for the women wear sleeveless summer dresses
and the men have taken off their jackets
but not their ties.
The women have bobbed hair and strings of beads,
the men, short-back-and-sides haircuts,
and they are all laughing.
It looks as though they have been playing cards,
since a flimsy folding table is
now covered with a cloth and teacups
and what remains of supper.

When I revisit this photo I'm struck
by the furnishings shown – 'Genoa velvet' armchairs,
a smoker's stand and a wireless set,
that ziggurat of shining bakelite, a glimpse
of a sideboard and what seems like
the edge of a traymobile.
What always puzzled me was why
the standard lamp in the background
displays a naked bulb, and now
I have just realised why they are laughing.
What I had thought an odd-shaped thing on the wall
is in fact the missing lampshade,
elaborate, fringed, and worn like a hat
by my mother.

This captured moment of silliness
affirms what takes so long to apprehend:
our parents once were young.

Leaf Shadows

i.m. my mother

When I think of you resting
in that sunny sitting room
it is always late afternoon.
Leaf shadows from the garden
are moving on the wall
and on a table near you
stands a pot of white azalea.
Light is spread on the polished floor,
motes hang in the air.
A chink of teacups pushed aside
and we fall silent.
That time of many conversations
is long gone. We tried hard
to shed reserve,
you dying, I still hoping
you were not.

Now that I lie in convalescent ease
remote from household noise,
leaf shadows on my wall
bring back the time –
the quiet room, the white flowers,
you so soon to leave us.

In the Picture

The bride and groom, their mothers,
the two bridesmaids,
the groom's brother and the bride's brother,
pose for this outdoor photograph.
The foreground is clear, the background misty.
It is London in September 1905.

The men wear top hats and high stiff collars.
The bride – solemn in her veil,
is holding lilies and carnations.
Unsmiling too the bridesmaids
in their large hats and muslin frocks.
Everyone looks glum.

Someone has laboured over the girls' dresses
and scrimped to pay for flowers.
Could the men have hired their hats?
Their frock coats? We shall never know.
And who has found the money
for this professional photograph?

All might pass quite unremarked except,
backdrop to the wedding group, is a high brick wall
spiked on top with shards of broken glass.

Lost Uncles

They still haunt us, these two young men who went to that great war
and did not come back. Thomas on my father's side, William on my
mother's. Lost uncles we never knew, enclosing a past we find it hard to
fathom, when England was called home and in the atlas half the world
was coloured pink.

Tom was middle brother of three, who all joined up together
– big farewell at the local church, where they all sang in the choir.
Flags and cheers, tea and cakes, rousing words from the rector
and sweethearts left behind. Commissioned early in the piece,.
he fell, badly wounded, in the battle of Fromelles. A soldier
moved him to a safer place, gave him water and sought help.
This much is recorded, along with the colour of his eyes and skin
and the list of his effects: pistol, clothes, tobacco pouch, a cane,
pocket chess and a New Testament, delivered to his family in the tin trunk
he left with. The girl he loved never married, became a courtesy aunt.

Will, seventeen years old, eldest but one of ten, handed a white feather
by a woman on the train, wrung from his mother consent to enlist.
Just eighteen when he sailed away, killed in action at Bullecourt
eleven months later. All that's left, a photo of a solemn, sweet-faced lad,
and pencilled letters to his mother, long-treasured in a metal box.
She is not to worry, his health is good and, would you believe,
he's an excellent shot! But the mud and lice are beyond belief.
Love to his brothers and sisters, he's sending postcards to the little ones.
When he gets home he'll have deferred pay; maybe twenty pounds,
so she must not fret about money, for this will help with the family.

Nobody knows where Tom and Will lie. At the time, Authority wrote,
in hope perhaps of cushioning the blow: *Particulars not to hand.*

Nursing Home

All day the old ladies
are kept in warm rooms.
The radiant screen confronts
their ruined circle
and brightness looms unflagging
as a world swims by – as far
away, unlikely and preposterous
as a star.

With rugs on knees
and food on trays
the days glide into night.
The nurses shout endearments
and, keeping nursery hours,
put out the light.

Evening

and the homeward bus is lurching
from the brightly lighted station
into the twilight, dreaming world
of wintry garden suburbs.
Smoke's in the air, and grass, and dinner.
The day goes out in a green sky
and the first star.

Soon the family men are heading
into their curving avenues,
smiling at the young girls passing,
soft as poppies in the night.
Keys turn in the fancy doors
and cymbal clap of saucepan lids
welcomes the hunter home.

The old-fashioned man in the turned-down hat
stumbles in at his laurel-dark gate
that warns of dogs long dead –
those were the days when the boys were young,
wore the lawn thin with cricket.
Dinner's to get and telly to watch
before he lies in his widower's bed.

Last off the bus, Miss Manifold,
the mainstay of her office,
with meat and vegetables in her bag
and tabloid murders for Mother,
who has sat all day in radioland,
knitting up little squares.

Now the empty bus rolls on
through the black suburban night.
The driver looks over his shoulder,
lights a fag and turns off the light.

Tears

How easily I shed them as a child,
in misery or frantic rage,
impervious to taunts of crybaby,
bawling my grief to the tiny world
which adults have forgotten
and only children know.

Nowadays I lay aside the melancholy book
with merely a sigh, sit stony-lipped
through many a tragic film,
not to mention global disasters
nightly served with the news
at dinner time. I meet
the loss of friends and loved ones
dry-eyed – albeit numb
with regret.

Almost I wish I had not lost the art
of weeping, lost the feel of warm tears
raining down my cheeks,
that collapse of control,
surrender to raw emotion.
But then I think: what could provoke
the breaking of this lachrymal drought?
And am thankful for
its continuance.

Dream

We did not see the bird at first.
It was dark on top of the wardrobe
but when the moon escaped the cloud
what seemed mere shadow moved
and the creature stretched its wings
in the light flooding our bedroom.

It was a very large bird with a beak
fierce as a petrel's. How had it got there?
We did not have time to wonder
for suddenly it took off and wanted out,
flying around the room, wings
wildly flapping, thudding against the ceiling,
hurling itself at the window.
'Quick, quick,' you cried and rushed
to open it more. 'I'll show it how.'
Next thing, you're clinging to the windowsill
with a forty-foot drop below.
Leaden-bodied, I could not throw off
the covers, cried out, and woke.
Woke you

When I went to the window
it was only open a crack
but a speckled feather
lay on the floor.

Skiing In the Main Range

In those days you could hire a 'cat'
and like a yellow tank it plunged
up and down the slopes and out
into the Main Range. We rocked around
inside, sliding down the narrow seats,
facing each other in our snow disguise.

Laughing, nervous, we clambered out
at the stopping place and sank
into fresh snow, struggling
to put on skis. Oh that day! Mountains
and meadows gleaming in the sun,
shadows as blue as the sky.

We had the ranges to ourselves
and the long run down Mount Townsend
lay before us. One by one we pushed off
and the swish of our skis was the only sound
as our trails turned the slopes
into a great expansive drawing.

Next morning I woke at dawn.
from a dream of an endless schuss
down Himalayan mountains.
Sometimes I was airborne,
flew lightly over crag and valley,
landed in a cloud of powder…

The lodge was buried in sleep.
Fresh snow had fallen in the night.
From my bunk the window framed
a piece of rosy sky, snowy ground
flushed pink, and gliding from the gums,
a red fox seeking food.

Forgetting

Good sometimes if I could forget,
but the memories persist.
I wish I could forget that old man
living in a drainpipe in Bombay
or the children near Madras,
a neat row on the roadside
smashing stones with hammers –
making what? Pebbles? Gravel?
Then there was the family
on a farmlet, the wife in a pink sari,
all smiling but knowing no English
as the guide explained
their poverty.

It would be good too to forget
those seaside villas in Dubai
and the hideous hotel atrium
(but not the afternoon tea)
and the voice of that German tourist
which sounded like traps
repeatedly snapped shut.

No forgetting either of
my past insensitivities,
the shaming gaffe,
the hurt received or given
and the failure to remember
what someone I loved
found memorable.

To an Adopted Child

I do not know
how you came to be,
the bodies mingled
at your making
quite unknown to me.
You came to earth
innocent as dew;
who decided
your disposing
I never knew.

Pity me, dear little child,
who gives you a name,
burdens you with my world
to which you made no claim.
We have no blood to bind us,
nor fleshly mystery,
only the hope of love
and the fact of our frailty.

Creature of myth and fable,
for so seems your birth to me,
when you reach understanding,
deal with me leniently.

Plastic Flowers

See how the tasteful arrangements
proclaim their permanence,
dewless and untender
as any furniture – yet very like:
tulip, apple blossom, rose,
lilies and delphinium,
scentless and their careful petals
dentless, something to be dusted
and kept nice.

My mother had a ball dress once,
crimson silk poppies
drowsy at the waist.
Crushed and spoiled at last,
they knew a kind of death,
their artifice did not outlive her.
So too the faded wedding wreath
and Parma violet hat,
unpretending ornaments that shared
a part of her mortality –
while these plastic beauties
still will bloom while
we decline, will meet
our last breath
with a bright stare.

Viewpoints

Seven years old and fearless,
I climbed to the top of the tree
in that green English garden,
pushing through curtains of leaves —
oak, sycamore – I forget which –
scrabbling footholds.
The lawn below disappeared
as from my perch the market town
spread before me, rooftops
steaming in June sunshine.
A train pulled out of the station
with a plume of smoke.
The church clock struck ten.
Small figures made their way
down High Street, a bus
came over the hill
and in the misty distance
I saw fields of watercress
by the river, but not
the mean terraces nearby.

These tiny houses on the edge of town,
the poor edge, said people
who didn't live there,
had always puzzled me.
It was not just the front doors
opening onto the street,
it was the doorsteps,
all of them scrubbed snowy white.
How, I wondered, could anyone
put a foot on such perfection?
How did anyone
get into their house,
let alone get out?
It was a long time before
I understood the importance of
an immaculate doorstep.

Sydney To Melbourne

If you didn't have a sleeper
on the old night train to Melbourne
they called it 'sitting up',
whether or not you reclined
with a cushion and a rug
and a paper bag of sandwiches
to savour in the dark.
Such was my childhood travel
returning to boarding school,
sleeping, waking, sleeping
and opening my eyes at dawn
to bleached and empty paddocks
stained with rosy light
and at melancholy intervals
a litany of dark blue hoardings
advertising *Dr Morse's
Indian Root Pills.*
What were they for?
And who was Dr Morse?
They haunted me
and seemed at one with the ache
of loneliness and longing
for family and home.

Place Dauphine

We found it again in late May,
more a triangle than a square,
where men played boules
on gravel under the plane trees.
The hotel's still there
but called something else.
It's clearly gone up in the world.

But this was where we stayed,
where all our friends stayed,
young and poor and hopeful,
bounding up the winding stair
to firetrap rooms sans bath
to marvel at our simply being
there, imagine – *in Paris*.

We saw the city, silver-grey,
the river through leafless trees,
and on dark early mornings,
lying close in our narrow bed,
heard cartwheels grind on cobblestones,
thought of tumbrils and the guillotine,
not cabbages, cheese and chickens
destined for Les Halles.

Starring in our own *Bohème*,
we heated our tin of soup
on a spirit stove safely placed
in the chipped enamel bidet
and retrieved a slice of Brie
from our mottle-mirrored wardrobe.
Cooking in rooms was forbidden,
an edict always ignored –
the place was full of students.

Breakfast came up three flights of stairs,
brought by an ancient maid,
panting from the bakery.
We ate our croissants full of guilt,
yet still wished they were hotter,
that she was younger
and could run faster.

V

Toast

First there is the smell.
You are coming into the house
after a bad day.
Probably it's cold and wet
and whatever you have been doing
has been unsuccessful.
But now you are greeted
with a warm fragrance.
Someone is making toast.
Your heart lifts. Someone loves you
and soon you will be spreading
good butter – it must be butter,
have no truck with margarine –
and as it melts deliciously
you will take your first bite.
Oh frabjous day! You are at one
with Mr Toad's delight
in buttered toast, treasured memory
from childhood reading.

Since it's such a part
of English-speaking culture,
Americans are good at toast;
unsurprisingly, Asians are not.
Europeans rarely attempt it
and certainly not for breakfast.
There is of course French toast
but that is really just an eggy conceit.
It is not proper toast.
Good toast naturally demands good bread,
firm of texture and robust in flavour.
Eschew anything resembling cotton wool.
Sourdough always answers well.

Some will assert the very best toast
is not made in an electric toaster
or even under a grill. No, it is made
with a toasting fork held
to the glowing embers of an open fire.
Thus spake Mrs Elizabeth David
and who would dare to disagree?

A Survivor

I love to wander in the Museum
of Australian food, to marvel
at endangered species or learn
of dishes now departed if not extinct.

What happened to carpet-bag steak,*
oyster soup, chokoes with white sauce,
salad dressing involving condensed milk,
or Spanish cream and puftaloons?#

Reassuring then to find a rare survivor,
the Australian spaghetti sandwich.
The pasta, soft little worms snugly nestled
in tomato sauce, still comes in small tins

that impart a faint metallic flavour.
This unique interpretation of spaghetti,
spread between slices of white bread,
finds its way to many a packed lunch.

What is more, it's still esteemed along
with a modest variation; heated and served
on buttered toast it can provide some consolation
for a humble, often lonely, evening meal.

---

* A steak stuffed with oysters.
# Puftaloons were scones deep-fried in dripping, often split and spread with golden syrup.

White

Quite a word – five letters to bear
such a load of meaning, source of suspicion
for those of colour, imperial burden
for those who were not. Symbol of virtue,
yet evil whitewashed, pallor of fear
or sickness, white noise for escapees
from tinnitus and the white feather
of cowardice often handed out to lads
in two world wars, so that many a mother's
white-haired boy joined up and died
at seventeen. Better to think of lilies,
white weddings and white ties,
clothes for cricket, tennis, white goods
for food and washing, white damask
for the table and white on white embroidery.
Better to remember white-water rafting
and the ocean's white horses or the
garden's white admiral butterfly.
Nor can I forget the gift I know will be
a huge white elephant, not to mention
the little lie I will tell when I receive it.

Red

Small word, so redolent of blood,
from the gaping wound to the rush,
unbidden, to the face in times of rage,
or the gentle blush of embarrassment.
Symbol of danger, light for stop and sleaze,
and may the greedy stay in the red
or be caught red-handed
with their fingers in the till.
And what a red-letter day
when the reds were not found
under the bed but the rednecks
all got their comeuppance –
ready or not.

Blue

Odd that this celestial hue painters
loved to fill with heavenly thrones,
attending angels, winged seraphim,
if not with tumbling mythic flesh,
odd that blue should give its name
to sadness and melancholy music,
legacy of slavery and the deep dark South.
Rather we marvel at that blue
from which come unexpected tidings,
nor do we ask why the bluebird
is the harbinger of happiness,
or the blood of aristocracy is blue.
We know to avoid bluebottles
so beautiful on the beach, and value
the blue heeler, that sturdy working dog
with whom it is unwise to ever
have a blue. We're used to blue-collar workers,
bluestockings and blue-eyed boys,
blue cheese, blue chips, even bluetooths,
but never question why ships leaving port
fly a flag they call a Blue Peter.
But for the bluest of all blues give me
the bluebag of vanished washdays –
the steaming copper, brimming tubs,
and that final rinse of ultramarine
before the sheets were fed to the wringer
and pegged on the line to flap and flaunt
their whiteness to the neighbours.

Yellow

Vincent did not have
a jaundiced view of yellow.
Consider that yellow self-portrait,
not to mention those sunflowers,
that furniture and those fierce
fields of wheat, and a blue night
swirling with yellow stars.
All dripped from his brush.
Nor did those emperors of Cathay
disdain a colour
they made their imperial own.
Oh those coats of yellow silk!
So why I wonder
are cowards considered yellow?
True, we're used to yellow fever
and once to yellow peril
but I'd rather dwell on yellow pleasures:
butter and eggs and yellow box honey,
wattles in bloom and poplar leaves
strewn on the ground in autumn,
while not forgetting the *fin de siècle* charms
of the Yellow Book or the wit
and sauce of Sydney's one-time
Yellow House.

Optimism

Every winter
I take out the knitting
never finished
I still hope
to find a child
it might fit
or maybe
someone to grow
into it

Mushrooms

Russian novels
are full of people
gathering them,
while wishing they
were in the city

Turkish Dessert

In Beatrix Potter's nursery
luncheon was always the same.
Grilled cutlet and rice pudding
was the name of the game.

Curious then to see so far
from Peter Rabbit and Tom Kitten
that in Turkey rice pudding is
constantly being eaten.

Every café has its puddings,
rows of them on display,
always burnt on top.
The Turks like them that way.

All that stuff about baklava
is really just – palaver.

Ten Tanka

in hospital,
always looking ahead
you made a drawing
of your files
to help me later on

old Emily
always had her canvas
flat on the ground
so desert flowers and yams
could grow from her brush

concert over
we take the ferry home
lights move
on dark water – gulls
white in the slipstream

ironing
in the late afternoon
only the hiss
of steam in the quiet room
as shadows lengthen

long white gloves
put away in tissue paper
waiting for
a bridal granddaughter
or St Vincent de Paul

café view
as we drink our coffee
a moving frieze
of umbrellas – Tokyo
on a wet Monday

early morning
grey and silver trees behind
curtains of mist
snug in the mountain cottage
we are eating buttered toast

how strange
to see tree ferns
bent with snow
and the rough red road
silent and white

everyone
is 'darling' at the nursing home
but someone
still managed to steal
my aunt's engagement ring

such virtue
to fill a cupboard
with marmalade
to know those lucent jars
mean my winter was well spent

Grace Cossington Smith's Interiors

How she loved doors!
Her interiors are full of them.
It's as if her front door has admitted us
to her house and the intimacy
of its rooms with their chests of drawers
and beds and chairs and sewing machine,
prosaic enough one would think,
except that all are suffused with colour.
And in the rooms are open doors
leading to her studio or the big garden
with its lawn and massed trees.
Then there are the wardrobes
with their open doors and mirrors
reflecting the veranda and more garden,
all awash with her signature brushstrokes
of multi-hued pigment
and the dazzle of light.

Open doors and open mind:
well-bred church-going spinster,
long-time resident of a genteel Sydney suburb
and early, amazing modernist.

Considering Fred Williams's Landscapes

Odd that we never
really noticed
how our trees look
straggling up a hillside,
ragged against the sky.
Until he showed us.

Farewell Claude and Constable,
Glover and Heysen too,
with your luxury
of form and light and shade,
noble trees and rolling cloud,
shining stream and the glow
of early evening…

No, we are set down
in amorphous scrub
on a scorching summer's day;
we are drenched in yellow ochre
scattered with what appear
to be random blobs of impasto.

Of course, there *is* light there
but it seems like
the unforgiving glare of noon.
Yet we could not be
more in this landscape.
Perhaps we'd always known
it in our bones — just needed him
to rip conditioning veils
aside.

Postcards

i.m. Terry

She had a gift for choosing cards
to send to friends – of whom she had
so many. Not just greetings

for Christmases and birthdays
but cards from where she travelled,
Paris often, or some unheard of place

she'd gone to seeking textiles.
There were cards of thanks for visits
or wishing you well for holidays,

funny cards and quirky cards she knew
would be enjoyed and sometimes
a card that introduced you to

an artist you didn't know.
Such was the last card she sent me,
a still life by Samuel John Peploe,

of whom I am ashamed to say
I did not know a thing. Scottish,
I learned, one of the Glasgow colourists.

I liked it so much I kept it
and meant to tell her so
but she died before I could.

Yet I'll always have her gift,
since she opened doors to pleasure
stretching beyond the grave.

Shrine

How they pile up
against the picket fence,
those tributes at the pop-up shrine,
messages and flowers
wrapped in cellophane,
soft toys and teddy bears,
companions for her journey,
faint bathetic echoes
of ancient rites.
Poor child,
we know your story
only too well,
unloved, disposable,
besotted mother
and the boyfriend
from hell.
After a decent interval
all will be cleared away
and the stain on the street
the neighbours feared
will gradually fade.
But the house
will be hard to sell.

VI

Fragments of a Life

from the unposted letters of Joseph Bergin

1. A Daughter's Note

When I went through Father's things*
I found so many letters
written and put away
in what looked like a biscuit tin.
He cannot have meant to post them,
for who would he send them to?
No name was ever given.
I felt such sadness reading them,
glimpsing the man I loved
moving among the words,
only partly seen
and only partly known.

---

* Joseph Bergin, my father and the writer of these letters, was a Polish Jew, well-connected, educated in Vienna and Paris, where it seems he had a brief love affair. An engineer, he arrived in Australia in 1950. After some time in a migrant camp at Boggabilla, NSW, he later worked on the Snowy Mountains Scheme, eventually forming his own construction company. He married my mother, an Australian, and had three children – myself and my two younger brothers. He ended his days immensely rich. I call them letters, for they are written on loose sheets of paper and seem addressed to someone, perhaps the woman he loved in Paris? Or maybe they were more a fragmentary journal?

2. Parting

When the night came you put on your coat,
left the old man by the stove
and sped through the frozen streets.
Snow fell on your scarf and on your lips,
your kisses were cold and when I took your hand
and warmed it in my own,
the lights streamed in our tears.
We found a café, drank some wine,
but could not think of much to say.
Were you remembering that meadow,
the poppies crushed beneath us as we lay
hidden in the long grass?
How long ago that seemed!
We parted. I to lodgings and the dragon's stare
as she handed me my key, and you
I pictured home again, helping him to bed,
and lying awake in the darkness beside him.

3. Cooma

The country here is broad and bleached.
open to the wind's knife; rocks
thrust through the earth's skin
like broken bones.
Skies are huge, snow clouds swell
and the cold grips like a vice.
There's a big fall in the mountains
but here it's sugar-sprinkled,
seldom lasting long.
Evenings and the town is full,
the pubs to bursting,
with men shouting, trucks revving,
sometimes fights. It's like
some sort of frontier, all fractured English,
everyone in gaudy parkas, woollen beanies,
snow-boots caked in mud.
In smoky cafés they're serving goulash,
steak and eggs, tomato sauce,
with beer in teacups, so they can't
be seen to break the law.
You would not like it here,
you would not like it here at all.

4. Café Culture

Erik, my friend from Boggabilla days,
has opened a café in Double Bay
and seems to be doing well
in spite of knowing nothing
of serving food and drink.
He says it helps that he's a count;
Magda does all the work,
he just concentrates
on exercising charm.
The women love it, he says,
if he clicks his heels and bends
as if to kiss their hands.

5. Householder

How you would smile to see me now,
living in a suburb, mowing a lawn,
trying to own a house like everybody else.
My wife is young and beautiful
but does not know it, has no idea
of setting out to charm.
She's so direct, so artless in her love
I love her all the more.
Not as I loved you and was consumed,
no, this is a quieter, gentler thing –
cups of tea together in the sun.
The baby's clothes whirl on a line
reminding me of carousels and music
churned from a Dutch organ.
On summer nights we sit on our veranda,
look for shooting stars and smell
the flowers that I have watered.
Me – a gardener! This European
so transformed! One thing, though,
I do not do – I never wash up.

6. Lost Ones

When I see my children's photos
smiling from the crowded page
I think of other carefree smiles —
the cousins of my childhood
lost to life in unknown camps.
I remember summers by the lake
and our woollen bathing suits
that took so long to dry,
lemonade and cake, eaten on the grass,
and nursemaids fussing with towels,
while the grown-ups in their deckchairs
smoked and laughed and said
that things would settle down.
I try not to think of Aunt Etta
with her ample figure exposed,
waiting, naked, in a line…

7. Housewarming

Well it wasn't quite a ball in Vienna
but we managed some chandeliers
and Betty wore her diamonds.
My wife has grown quite European
as I've grown less. It's strange,
the house is bigger and better
than any we've had before
and yet she still seems wistful,
as if she wanted more.

The guests streamed through the rooms,
were suitably impressed before
they stepped into the garden
where they'd put up a marquee.
Betty was pleased with the food
but had to speak rather sharply
to a waiter at the bar.
Our boys had a bit too much to drink
but our darling daughter did not.
Something in her curtained look,
shy, yet self-contained, reminded me of you.

Later, I stood at the harbour's edge
enjoying the slap of water on the wall
and the warm scent of the sea,
when fireworks flooded the sky
and a sudden flush of pearly light
fell on the upturned faces of my friends.
I remembered the cousins and poor Aunt Etta
and my eyes filled with tears.

8. The Vacant Bed

Such a long dying! Cruel to see
her beauty wasted, her eyes
a plea for death.
Pots of white azalea
on a table near her bed
framed her yellowed face.
Holding her hand, I felt
my touch could crush
her little bird-like bones.

Now her door is shut, the bed empty,
the wardrobes are full of clothes
and her brush and comb
still on the dressing table.
The scent she used lingers.
Her diamonds are in the safe.

9. The Painting

I ended the meeting early today
and went to buy my painting.
Such an odd little picture,
by no one anyone's heard of.
Young, I suppose, just starting,
hinting at landscape, colours
of ochre, indian red and black.
It made me remember the smell
of dry grass and burnt trees
all those years ago when first
I came to this country.
They were very polite at the gallery
but puzzled at my purchase –
they'd hoped I'd buy the Brack.

10. Leaving

She has wheeled me onto the terrace,
with a rug to keep me warm.
I'm to look at the boats and ferries
until it's time for tea.
'There you go', says my bosomy,
not to say bossy, nurse.
She gives me a friendly pat.
I control my irritation;
she means well. They all mean well.

www.ingramcontent.com/pod-product-compliance
Lightning Source LLC
Chambersburg PA
CBHW070935080526
44589CB00013B/1519